A Devilish Tale

First published in Australia in 2006.
Reprinted 2008, 2012 by Alice Hansen,
Hobart, Tasmania, Australia

Email: alice@alicehansen.com.au

This work is copyright. All rights reserved.
No part of this publication may be
reproduced, stored in a retrieval system
or transmitted in any form by any means
without the prior written permission of
the publisher and copyright holder.

National Library of Australia
Cataloguing-in-Publication data:

Author: Hansen, Alice, 1980.
Title: A devilish tale.
For preschool children.
ISBN 0 9802800 0 1 (pbk).
1. Tasmanian devil – Juvenile fiction. I. Title.
Dewey Number: A823.4
Produced in Tasmania, Australia

Cover design: Lea Crosswell
Editing: Impress: clear communication

Technical/creative support:
Simon Hansen, Ian Wallace/ Will Whitehouse,
Bridget Fuglsang & Georgia Innes

Printed in China by 1010 Printing Limited

A devilish
tale

When Nevil the Devil woke up to the sparkling Tasmanian day he was all alone.

He had fallen asleep after playing follow-the-leader. Chasing his brother's tail had worn Nevil out.

All that remained of Mummy and Daddy Devil was a faint scent.

Where has his family gone?

He walked down a long path, following the sound of crashing waves.

Nevil had never seen a beach before.

The sand was so soft!

Flicking it about with a devilish chuckle he nearly forgot he was all alone at Wineglass Bay.

Then he started to feel very lonely.

The trees looked much bigger now that Mummy and Daddy Devil were not here to protect him.

The path twisted and turned, leaving Nevil spinning in circles.

After a long walk Nevil came across a giant lake.

He would have to use all his devil might to cross it.

A clever little devil, he made a bark canoe and used a stick to paddle.

Ripples swept across Dove Lake and rocked his canoe.

His tail slipped into the icy water.

Would Nevil make it to shore?

Yes! Nevil made it to dry land just as snow began to fall.

He started to shiver and wished for his cosy family den.

Nevil had never seen snow falling from the sky.

He thought it might be his mother's milk being sent from above.

He opened his mouth but the snowflakes disappeared when they touched his tongue.

Nevil heard noises coming from some giant creatures he had never seen before.

He hid as his mother had taught him.

When the big legs disappeared, Nevil saw a delicious apple left behind.

What a delight!

Nevil found himself in a deep, dark hole. When Nevil screeched in fear, he heard another screech come back!

Did this mean his family were in Hastings Caves?

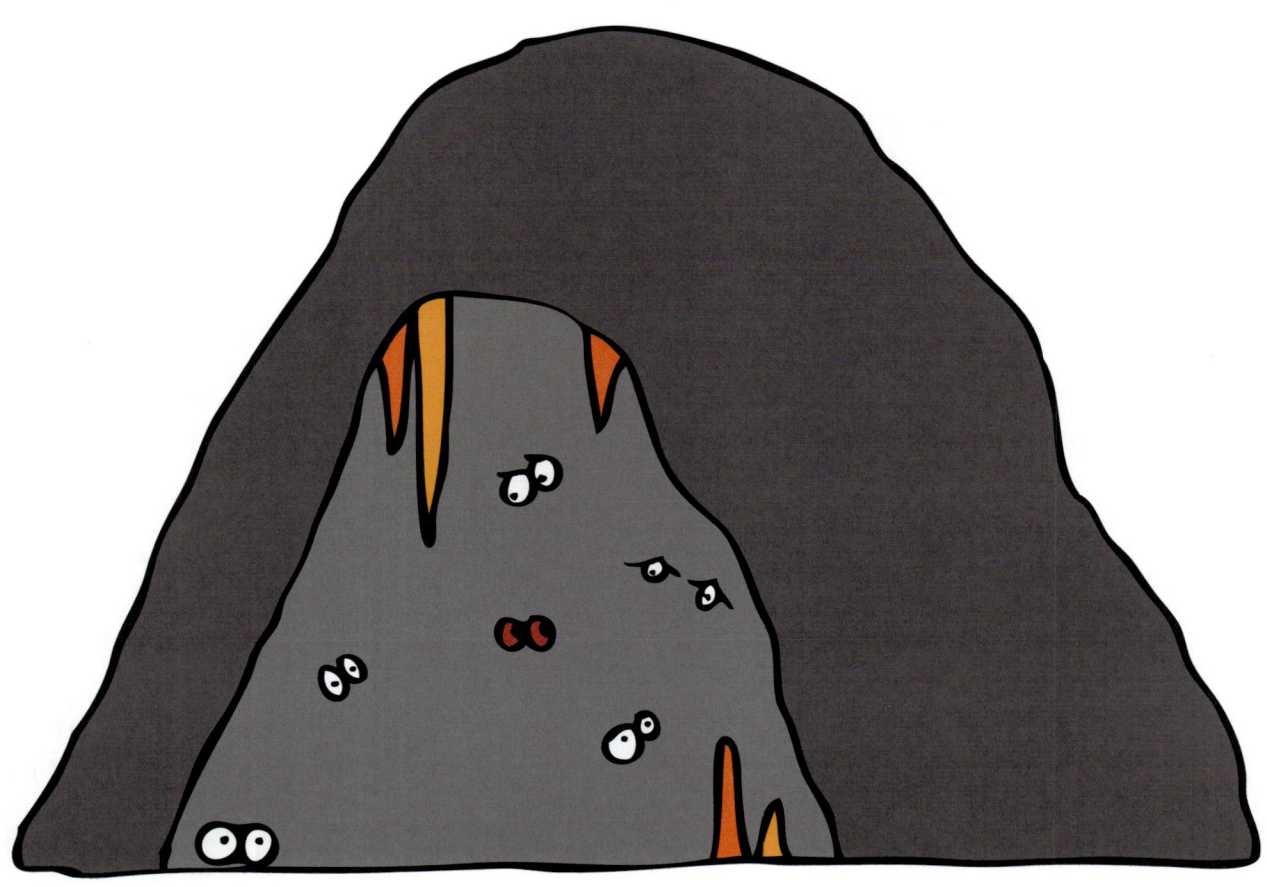

"Do not be scared," a friendly glow worm said.

"I live down here. Your family are not here, little devil. It is your echo that you hear."

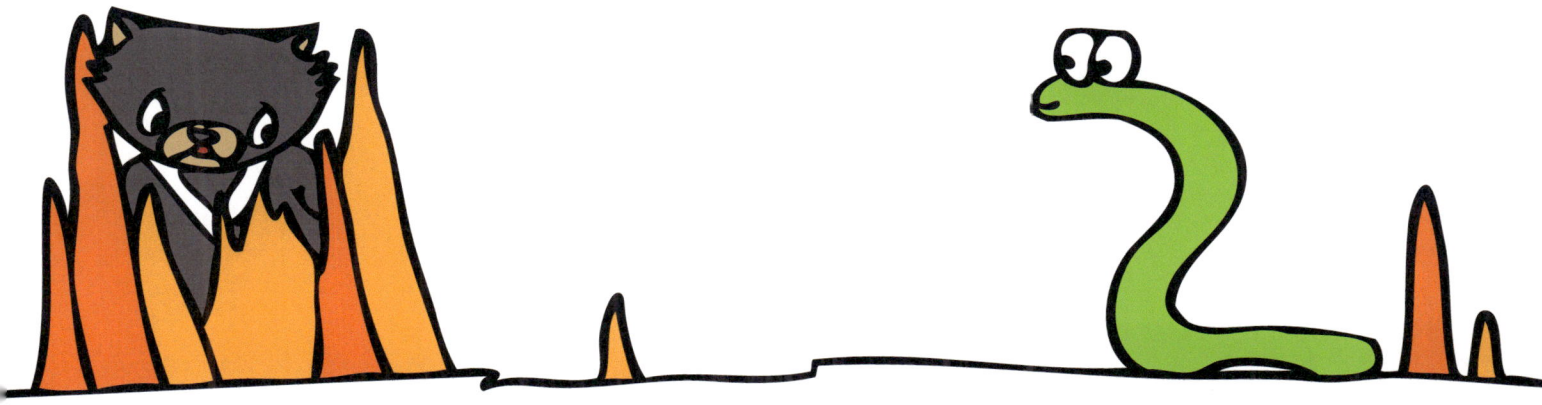

Was he ever going to find his family?

Nevil cried so much that his paws could not stop the tear drops. The tears ran into a giant waterfall.

Nevil thought that the wet slippery-slide might take him to his family. He jumped into the streaming water.

Would it carry him home?

"Welcome to Wallaby Land," came a friendly voice. "You seem lost."

"I can not find my family," sniffled Nevil. "Can you help me?"

"Hop in my pouch and I will take you to the Wise Old Wombat," said Mrs Wallaby.

With a bounding leap, Nevil was on his way again.

Mrs Wallaby stopped at the burrow and said sternly,

"Don't disturb his dreamtime. Wait for him to come out."

The Wise Old Wombat soon came out, and sure enough he knew a trail home.

Nevil skied across Henty Dunes.

He giggled with glee as sand flew up behind him.
"I am going home," he sang. "Weeee!"

Nevil followed Wise Old Wombat's directions but something blocked his way along the west coast...

Nevil could see deep water underneath him.

Had the Wise Old Wombat led him to a dead-end?

Was his family across the ocean?

Of course not!

His mother had told him that Tasmania was the only place in the world that devils liked to live.

He just had to climb a mountain to get home.

The cliffs were steep and dangerous for little Nevil.

He saw a strange lizard.

"What have you been eating? You have a funny blue tongue," said Nevil.
"I am a blue-tongue lizard," he replied. "I have food for us to share."

Nevil made sure that dinner had not turned his tongue blue and continued on his way.

Nevil was at Port Arthur now, around big old buildings.

A giant creature, called a human, scooped up Nevil and put him in a cage.

He was taken to what the humans called a Wildlife Park.

When he got there he heard a voice that he knew very well ...

"Nevil, it is Grandpa Devil," it croaked.

"I live in here now. I am not well and the humans take care of me. Your family lives just over that creek. Jump out of the cage and run to them, little devil!"

Nevil smiled and dashed away.

He was so excited that he jumped right over the creek.

Sure enough there was his family.

They all screeched with happiness.

"Young Nevil," exclaimed Mummy Devil, "where the devil have you been?"

"If I told you, you would think I was telling devil tales," said Nevil.

"How about a game of follow-the-leader? I will not let that tail out of my sight this time!"

The Tasmanian devils are suffering from a rare facial tumour disease which is threatening the species. No less than $10,000 profit from this book will be donated to the Tassie Devil Appeal run through the University of Tasmania.

Made in the USA
Columbia, SC
07 December 2023